REINCARNATION OR INVADING SOMEBODY ELSE'S BODY

WRITTEN BY.
BISHOP JAMES T. JOHNSON

authorHOUSE®

AuthorHouse™
1663 Liberty Drive
Bloomington, IN 47403
www.authorhouse.com
Phone: 1 (800) 839-8640

Published by AuthorHouse 03/01/2017

ISBN: 978-1-5246-7393-2 (sc)
ISBN: 978-1-5246-7392-5 (e)

CONTENTS

FOREWORDS

In this book the Author,is simply displaying that reincarnation is really real people have really over looked that God is really a diverse God. God is not someone who just throws people in Hell because they lived a sinful,life style thats what christians have been taught,but it is the principle of God any thing can happen..from my experiences with dealing with reincarnation,many people who have died have really had another chance to come back and live another life so that they can get there lives back together,with the almighty God who has many many names.. I can tell you that from my own experience in dying and being able to come back again in another body,to live once more so I can make things right with the one true God that has many,names.so what im saying once again is that reincarnation is very real.... in this wonderful book you will learn so many life changing things...

CHAPTER 1

Do you believe that reincarnation is real ???

Yes alot of people do not believe that reincarnation is real, yes it is real most christians will never believe that its real only the people who have been threw it will believe that it is real. Yes good people of God he did ordain reincarnation,most of you that are reading this book right now have been here on this earth more than one time. Most people just deny it,because it's just not logical for them to believe.That the God that they pray to would do such a thing,it doesn't matter who you pray to as long as it's not the devil it's all the same God.. Who created all life God does what he wants to do when he wants to do it. If he wants to reincarnate his people he will do so,nothing will stop him anyway.Some people want experience any dealing in there life time with reincarnation. They just go on living there life how they wish to do it,denying all existent of everything.Reincarnation is not something abnormal its something,most people will go threw so that if you messed up in your first body you can get a second chance to make things right again. God is bigger than the bible describes him as, he is so lenient towards the people that he put here on this earth,and he is in know ways ready to end this earth no time soon.so stop being worried about judgement day,its not coming no time soon,as I said earlier most of you have been here on this earth so many times that you have forgotten count.I myself know for a fact that I have been here four times.There is know telling how many more times I will come back to vsit the people in the earth realm,remember theres nothing like having life in your own body ..may your reincarnation journey be very blessed and a enjoyable one.....

CHAPTER 2

What is Reincarnation ???

(Definition for Reincarnation is.... The belief that the soul,upon death of the body comes back to earth in another body or form.

   now the question is do you believe it or do you think its not real. I can tell you from my own experience that it is true I myself have been here 4 times,and I dont know how many more times that I will come back,before I go to rest. Most of you dont know or will you believe that (God) Himself is responsible for this thing happening to you and for a good reason.(KJV Bible Isaiah 55.8 & 9... For my thoughts are not your thoughts, neither are your ways my ways saith the Lord.... For as the Heavens are higher than the earth,so are my ways,and my thoughts than your thoughts. AMEN. Now by that being said that tells you that God does what he wants to do,when he wants to. So you dont need to try to figure him out,because you never will God is in charge and the Holy Bible only gives a scratch of who he really is in other words God is Infinite meaning everlasting like a duracell battery. Reincarnation is Gods plan for his people,just because it does not talk about it in a direct way in the Bible does not mean its not real..I to once was blind but now i can see,it took God to open my eyes so that I would not miss a beat,because im a very mystical person myself the spirit,realm is my domain all day and week long,I know more about Reincarnation than the average man or women.

CHAPTER 3

When people die where do they go ???

That is a really good question,most people believe Heaven or Hell that is not the case all the time even though it can happen. Im sure that many many things has happen as I told you God is very diverse he will not allow man to figure him out no matter what happens. You will know right then where your going to Heaven or Hell, just because you think someone else is going so please do not judge. Once again we're talking about reincarnation.Most people when they die choose to jump in and out of bodies especially there love ones,they do not go very far.Thats probably very hard to swollow,but it is very true God is not overly excited about just putting someone in hell,Im sure he is excited about putting people in heaven,but not hell bound status.That's why most people that die do reincarnate,Boodism religion speaks on it alot but some christians do not believe in it.as the word of God tells us you will perish for the lack of knowledge.My good people there is a Heaven and Hell but you need not to focus in on it,because life is the way that it is.God is really compassionate,towards his people and he will allow most of you to reincarnate.Christians I need you to get on board with me,so I can teach you all about you,and one of the real way's God truly works..God Bless

----

CHAPTER 4

Is there a Heaven & Hell ???. If so then who goes there ???

There is alot of ruckus about who is God and who is right or wrong in this world that we live inregards of who is going to judge the sinners and the righteous. Well let me clear my throat on that particular question,so that you will understand,you will be judged by your heart,did you love everyone and did you treat everyone with kindness,also did you judge people instead of trying to help them. That's Heaven and Hell it is the work that you put in. That will determine where you go amen.Now let's get to it,we are talking about reincarnation this is where when people die they come back in another body or someone else's body which is hard to grasp for alot of people,as I said in the earlier part of this book.when people die they have a choice to jump in and out of other people's bodies are go sit in the light.Most of them will not choose to go to the light because they will want to be with want to close there love one's.Then again who can blame them because the average person does not want to die,they want to live allday long. You will know right then when you die if your going to Heaven or Hell when you come out the body. what confuse alot of people is they do not believe that God allows us to do it. so many people write about reincarnation,it's only there knowledge of what they know I can not tell you if what there saying is true or not everyone know what they have experienced or not experienced so I can not say that someone else is wrong are right, I just Know what I have experienced.The Rap guy's want to know is there a Heaven for a gangster,all I can say about that is I have seen everything else,It might just be a heaven for just Gangsta's..(LOL) God does what he want he wants to do,and how he wants to do it Amen. So many people live in fear about where are they really going I will tell you it is a great possibility that you will reincarnate until you get it right so you can enter into the gates of Heaven unless you just want to go to the pit of Hell with the devil and his fallen angels.

CHAPTER 5

Can Spirits Invade Someone Elses body ???

Spirits are allowed by God to invade someone else's body by the will of God, why he allows it I do not have that answer, but I can guarantee its for a good reason. I have seen father's that died jumped into the daughters body and live there until her death, that's exactly will happen if someone like myself does not show up to get them out of the body,I can tell you that when I show up on the seen your time is probably up in the body that you have taken over.This has been going on for many many years,probably isnt going to change. When these spirits Invade these bodie's they can do some things there most favorite thing to say to me is they need me I was the one who made them strong. The spirit has control over the body some type of way,but it does not want to let people know that they are there in that body. All of them tell me when I ask them did they know that they could jump into someone's body they all say the same thing no I did not know.Alot of you that are reading this book now did not know,I mean its not a big secret most of you dont know because you do not want to know.You wait until your dead then your trying to come back to be with your family some type of way, and the best way you found out was to jump into your love one"s body. Right now many of you are saying to yourselves. that this is a bunch of silly talk but some of you really know that this is real stuff,besides everything in this book I can back it up with proof.

many of you right now that are reading this book your love one could be in your body right now,reading this book with you and you would not even know that it was happening. When they enter your body are you can call it,Invading your body if you want to I dont care,these spirits can feel and taste what you feel and taste. The spirit becomes one with you even though your are two different spirits.It's like a root being placed in your body,believe it or not some of those spirits really do help people get threw there rough times in there lives. Some of them hurt people when they believe that its there body and not the actual person body that there in.Then God has to send some one like me to pull the spirit out of the body,all I do is bring temporary judgement,to the spirit under the leadership of God who is (CHRIST OUR LORD AND

SAVIOUR). Im allowed to send the spirit to the light to rest,or chain the spirit to darkness. This judgement by me is until judgement day,the spirit will remain there until God comes to judge them

----

CHAPTER 6

How do you Invade somebody Elses Body ???

The number one thing you should know is these spirits that are Invading somebody elses body is ordained by God himself,most of you will probably never believe it,especially if your a christian most christians only believe whats on in the Bible,whats self explaniority if its not saying something that they can't understand they dont want nothing to do with it.That's what makes them very Ignorant now dont get things confused Im a christian myself one hundred percent,and thats all I will ever be.. Amen. But right now were talking about spirits Invading somebody"s body I know most people get afraid when they hear that but just know that no one really dies they just leave the body and most of them not all of them set right there watching their family the entire time,that you no there dead.All they can think about is getting back to there old life in the flesh you see thats when it becomes real when you are dead and there is nothing else that you can do for your family are your children from the spirit realm side. This is how they are able to jump into bodies,from there burning desire to get back to there love ones. God allows them to enter the bodies of there love ones,and they live another life threw them as long as they can but most of the time the person that body there in do not even know that there love one is in there body. Living there life again threw there love one sounds to crazy doesnt it I know it does I did not know until the Lord showed it to me I was praying to God who is CHRIST JESUS THE THE LORD ALMIGHTY. I asked him to up my power,because I was just use to casting out devils I was very famous for it, then one day in church service I asked one of the spirits in the body of a lady who are you,generally it would say satan or Lucifer, or kill or murder,something in that nature now this particular time the spirit said my name is Johns and I said John who,I was curious because all the years that I had been casting out devils I had never heard of a demon named John. So I said how did you get in that bdy he said I died 20 years ago in a car crash,in Iowa I went off a clif of a bridge I was drunk,and I was killed in the car crash so I have been jumping in and out of bodies every since that night 20 years ago.Of course I had to say how do you do that he said the devil showed me how to do it,and everyone else is doing it as well,so now you know how people are Invading somebody elses body,as I told you nothing is done without the permission of the Lord.It was new to me and a big big,shocker to me but be careful what you ask for you just might get it. You can call me the ghost buster,because all I mostly encounter in bodies now that God has allowed to happen is people who are deceased and they are jumping in and out of bodies daily but they do find a body to reside in for a while,If they so decide to take over that body in a file way thats when I step in and send them to the light or chain them to darkness,until judgement day.

CHAPTER 7

Spirits just want to talk ???

Most of you do not understand the mission that a spirit has when they are in the spirit,realm they cannot communicate the way that they want to so they just roam back and forth to and forward. Most of them just want to talk but they do know,that if they speak threw the body of someone they just might find someone to get them out of that body.Thats what they do not want so they dont want to expose themselves in the body,but they do want to talk.They want things to be just like it was when they were living. But we all know that it will never be the same like that again unless the Lord reincarnate them,threw another wound of a woman to be reborn again,in the normal process that they went threw being born the first time. When they start talking they dont want to shut up. all they want to be is seen just like everybody else who is actually breathing threw a body. They will also tell who killed them as well if the murder case is not solved,I have had a few tell me who killed them,it is quite amazing how this entire thing works when it comes to the spirit realm,they are always watching us on this side they never rest they never sleep,all they do is roam. It will be that way until the end of time,God has ordained things to be this way and at the same time he protects us from just walking around all day long seeing dead people all day and night long.As I said all they want to do is just talk I know I make it sound very simple but it really is simple,you can not change the way things are I have spoken to celeberties who have passed on,the most two Interesting ones to me were (Marilyn Monroe) & (Princess Diana) they had alot to say about there lives when they were living, I even spoke to actress from the 1960's (Sharon Tate) she spoke about charles Mansion how he murdered them. I had never even heard of Sharon Tate,I did not know who she was until she surfaced up,in that persons body that I was dealing with but after the session was over I of course looked her up,and it was the same story that she had told me that the whole world already new about.The most Intresting thing that hit my spirit was when Marilyn Monroe & Sharon Tate said they were burning in Hell until a light came and pull them out and from that moment they were allowed to jump in and out of peoples bodies . Especially the ones who showed lots of energy for her,they can feel who has that energy for them... so watch your energy that you may have for the dead they just might visit you.

CHAPTER 8

Solving Unsolved Mysteries & Murder's ???

This is where it gets a little Intresting when it comes to spirits coming back from the dead to tell who killed them,its like a lifetime movie or a hollywood movie where you see the physic,go into a trance mode and he or she see everything that happened to whom ever that got killed. This is when the murder of them is not solved, and it is true they do come back to tell who killed them if they can find someone with my ability,0r you may say physic ability its whatever you want to call it but it is all a gift from the Lord up above. Even in death people still want to talk they just dont have there human flesh to do it in anymore so they have to find a Host,meaning a body to talk threw. For years its been done this way,if the spirit can find someone that has the power to hear them and communicate with them. They will talk and not all of them are evil, they just want to communicate again with this earth realm,so many people out there are so afraid of the dead that the dead has been misenterpreted,so many different ways that it has made the dead look like they are really bad but all it is,they just have left there physical bodies and they are trying to communicate with the living and it is ordained by God himself. Let me make myself clear when I say God his name is (JESUS) as I said earlier in this book christians are the ones that turn everything around the way they want it to be,and nobody elses opinion matters. (CHRIST) has sent me to straighten things out about life after death or you can call it reincarnation life style,but either way it goes its still ordained by (CHRIST) Everything that you do in the land of the living your being watched by a spirit,rather if the spirit is good or bad,everyone of them have a story to tell,if you can imagine what im doing in writing this book,all im doing is representing the dead because they have been misunderstood, and I was born for this purpose God has many many avenues about him that you do not know about are you dont care to know about,because you are simply afraid. Even in death they still mnage to tell someone who did it to them even if they haft to enter the body of someone to show them the hidden evidence, I bet you did not think that way did you because they can invade other peoples bodies and try to do what ever they want but there is a guideline to everything. God will only allow them to go so far with there attempt to take over the body completely and in some situations they do take over the body and thats when I come on the scene to correct all of that as I said Im the Ghost Buster,and the spirits know my authority, they obey it just as we do the police ine the land of the living,just remember that they can invade police detectives and lead them to the evidence thats needed to solve cases, or they can take them over and walk them right to the right person who committed the murder.

CHAPTER 9

The difference between dead people and Demons ???

There is a difference between dead people and demons,a lot of people who don't have my information can easily get it mixed up. Even pastors who deal in deliverance of demons in people can get it mixed up as well.Because they dont have the extra gift as i have or someone else may have,you can easily think that because you got the demon spirit out the person they will return back to normal,but that is not the case when a spirit is behind the door you will think it is a demon because the signs and symptons will look the same have you ever heard of the expression dont judge the book by its cover,are all of certain people look a like it is a assumption, that can really fool you.It is a very fragile situation,when it comes to dealing with demons and spirits,now let me explain to you the difference between, a demon and a spirit. A demon is a demonic force that works for the devil himself in other words demons are falling angels who went bad in the Heavens and God punished them and kicked them out of Heaven and renamed them demons. Spirits are people who were once alive living on this earth as humans,so when a human dies they are called spirits. We have heard many stories about people seeing spirits in there house,or in hospitals,jails,or just walking around there houses. You just about see them any where you go if God allows you to see them but they are people who died and left there bodies and now are spirits are you can call them dead people.As I said in the beginning of this chapter a deliverance preacher can get it mixed up,very easily trying to know whats a demon or a spirit. Spirits can cause the same affect in the body as a demon spirit,so it really can confuse you the demon is going to have a different name than the spirit,because they are in two different categories but will have nearly the same function and affect. Both spirits and demons can enter you threw a bloodline curse and they both can be in your body at the same time,and both can cause real trouble in your life because both of them,are trying to take over your body,and use you for there purpose.I know it sounds really strange to you but its been going on since the beginning of time that God created the earth. Some of you cant believe that your reading something like this but it is real as it will ever be I have been dealing with this form of life style for a very long time I have come up with this information to share with you, so you can better help yourself and help someone else.Both of these two entitees can invade your body by being summond threw a VOODOO, HOODOO, WITCHCRAFT SPELL, and both of them will be in your body at the same time,I have seen people who practice witchery put these spirits and demons in the body of people just because they did not like them,and it messed up ther lives until I came along and pulled them out. The first thing that I do is ask the spirit in the body who are you and when it gives me its name I can determine then if its a demon or spirit,and from that point I will proceed to ask it how it got in that body,and it will always tell who sent it to that body. I question the spirit like the police would do in there interagation room,and after I get my whole entire story of what happened then I start the punishment process are reward process because every spirit in that body could not be bad but was just looking to live again, but the demons I send all of them to the pit of Hell in the name of (JESUS) Amen......

CHAPTER 10

Can someone die in the 1800s
and resurface in the 1900s
in there new body ???

Yes it is very possible for that to happen and it is happening every day, as I said most of you will not even know that you lived a life before the one that your living now. What happens is the Lord will wipe your memory,and he does that for a good reason so that your former life will not enter fear, with the one your living right now. Some of you may have died 100 or 200 years ago and now your back,living another life right now in this time zone. Whats so fascinating about it is your back in your new body the body is yours not someone elses body,God has allowed you to reincarnate so your back again to get your life right so that the next time that you die you will hopefully be done pleased the Lord so that,you can enter the gates of HEAVEN where the Father in HEAVEN sits up high and looks down low amen. I know this is probably a little hard to swallow but it is true I have been back here a few times myself and each time I come im in my own body not Invading somebody else's body. As I told you this is Ordained by God and this will continue to go on as long as this earth keeps turning. Some people even myself you may start having a few flash backs about the last life that you lived,now remember this is past events about your past life not someone elses I seen a TV Show once that was coming on for one season,they were telling people that they had pass lives and the truth was those spirits in those bodies that he was pulling up were spirits of people who had died,and had jumped in there bodies so the person that was telling the TV audience that those people were seeing there past life events,they were actually the spirit in the body of that person who was coming up and talking about there past life not the person who he had put in a trance. So the whole entire audience that was watching the TV Show was actually deceived but things like this happen when people just don't know,and as the show would come to a end he would research those people who they said they were and some times find them but as I said that was the spirit in there body talking not the past life of that person,so he would ask them do you think that it was your past life and of course all of them,said yes I do.. not knowing what was going on.

CHAPTER 11

Can you communicate with your Love one's who has passed on ???

Many people desire to communicate with there love one's that has passed away and it is possible to communicate with them number one if your not afraid, because that would cause a big communication problem because the love one already know that your going to be afraid if they just showed up to you out of the spirit realm,your going to panic and possibly hurt yourself. But if the love one has a gift from God who name is (JESUS) has given you a gift to actually see them and to feel them around you the love one who is deceased is going to know that you,have that gift so they will try to communicate with you the best way that they can if you have a incredible strong gift they will be able to communicate with you on a level that will be stronger than the person who does not have a gift.It will be like more of a psychic level and thats where Im at in my life with this entire situation,but Im not a psychic Im a Ordained Minister of the Gospel for JESUS. And im pretty good at communicating with the other side which we call the dead people who some how scare the living life out of most people,who are living in the flesh. With my special ability that God has given me im able to control spirits in every realm, meaning the spirits in africa will be different than the spirits in america,they both have a different vibe the spirits in africa seem to be more agressive than the spirits in america. But I have the power and ability to control spirits from the Heavens and from Hell,I can call them up how I want to call them up I dont care if its from JFK. to sammy Davis JR. I have the power to throw them in bodies of people and allow them to speak threw there bodies.the spirits they know it thats why when I do seminars on reincarnation they know where im going to be,so they can start jumping in the body of there love ones are anybody body that they can get into to speak with me because they know that I have a very strong communicating gift,to speak with them and I have no fear of them because they just want to be heard as well as a person who is alive. Also God has allowed them to have a voice on the other side,I spoke with many spirits that told me they were trying to take care of there families even from the other side. Yes its overwhelming to hear something like that coming from the dead so that tells you they are just as much alive as the living people are. God has made me and some others to be the voice for his deceased children,so that they can have a voice as well from the other side remember when JESUS came MERCY came as well and it even means MERCY unto the dead as well. So many people are at my door communicating with there love ones from the other side so they can feel that they are still connected with the love one who has left the body,so remember dont be afraid just communicate with them the best way you can are just give me a call I will help you in the process in communicating with your love ones remember there not dead ther just out of there flesh.... AMEN

CHAPTER 12

Can the human eye see dead people and hear them and smell them ???

The (HOLY BIBLE) speaks of different gifts that God gives his people,and everyone of us has a spiritual gift from the Lord. Go to the book of (1st Corinthians 12.9)it speaks of a gift called (discerning of spirits) with that gift you can see and hear dead people and also smell them.All these things are ordained by god now you can stop wondering why your going threw what your going threw,you have a gift rather if you want it or not you were born with it so you may as well just use it for the good of the Lord. Some of you are called and some of you are chosen,the ones that are chosen as I am myself your going to be the one's who go threw the most because god has chosen you to do great things,those spirits know who you are they know your power and also they know your purpose that God has given you so you can stop trying to hide. These gifts will not just fade away you will fade away before the gift will you were put on this earth so serve the Lord and nothing else. Let's talk about the gift of seeing dead people they will always appear to you because of your gift you will get a lot of glimpse of spirits especially when your not expecting to see them thats when they show up,they are always watching you because they don't sleep as you and I do.It can also happen,when your just waking up at night are doing the morning hours you will see someone standing there watching you of course most of you jump up running because your afraid of what you don't know about. Some of you will hear them calling your name are hear them,just yelling in the spirit realm your most quite time you will probably hear things moving around in the back room,hitting the walls are just singing in the spirit realm because there just trying to get your attention most of them don't mean you no harm its just that they know that your gifted. You will also smell them as well it will smell like the perfume are cologne that they use to wear when they were living you will smell it. They do that on purpose so you will know that they are still with you watching you day and night,there is nothing that you can do but pray to God to give you the understanding about your gift and please stay in prayer it will bless you.

CHAPTER 13

Is it a gift when a person can speak to the dead and control them???

Is that a big question yes or no I will let you decide that one for yourself,ok I will answer it for you yes it is a gift when a person can speak to the dead. In the Bible the Book of (John 11.43 & 44) Is where JESUS called into the spirit realm of the dead to raise lazarus who had already been dead about four days.You really need to be opened minded about this entire situation if not you will be looking like this guy is crazy,but it is a true fact that JESUS spoke to the dead and my words to the world is why not he controls the Heavens and Hell,he is almighty you can imagine how I felt when I started communicating with spirits it was a different moment for me in regards of dealing with them,remember as long as your communicating with them you are in charge. One thing about being able to speak to them is your in control that is ordained by God,they know it so you should know it as well,they will try to scare you into not using your authority that God has given you.As I said most of these spirits just want to talk they have there own agenda I have spoken to some spirits that tell me they are not dead,because they are just arrogant like that they probably were arrogant when they were living.These spirits act the same way in the spirit realm that they acted when they were alive,I have spoken to some of them that acted the same way in spirit I got that evidence in a service once the cousin of the spirit were in my service who knew him,the first thing they said was when he came up talking was (wow)he acts the same way in the spirit as he did when he was living. Now to me that was amazing because just when you thought that the devil who is very stupid had something to do with everything actually it was the person. By the way im not giving the devil no respect because he is our only enemy,and that will never change.I hope and pray those of you reading this book is getting a great deal of information out of this book that you will be blessed by the teaching because I wrote it for you to educate yourselves on whats going on in the spirit realm...

CHAPTER 14

Carriers... Who are they & what are they ???

This chapter here is really going to help you define whats really going on in your life,and the life of your love one's because alot of you did not know that God,allowed some people to carry spirits in there bodies and its ordained by God. Yes I said chosen by God to carry spirits in there bodies the reason why is because they all have a message to give to the people.Most of you have never heard of a carrier,especially when it comes to reincarnation its a topic that some people don't want to hear any way but it does not matter I have a job to do and I shall complete my task .About fifty percent of the people on this planet are carriers of spirits and they may not even know it or dont really care but most people have spirits of people who are dead living in there bodies,most of these are your own family members who have passed away,and when they came out of there body they found out lots of things that possibily were not told to them,when they were living. Number one is that you have a option to go to the light or roam the earth realm and jump in and out of bodies until the end of time thats when the judgement is passed down from God himself.Exactly what are carriers they are people who are very special to God,the lord allws spirits to invade there bodiesfor his name sake.God lets you know that he is in charge of the dead and the alive,all they want to do is talk. sometimes they can go over board with there old ways from when they were living,it is a surprise to the person that is deceased that when they die that they are able to jump in and out of bodies of there love ones.You could be a carrier of spirits and dont know it,doctors diagnose you with mental Illness,Bipolar & schizophrenia. But whats really going on is all those spirits in the body that have taken over the body and it will run you crazy if God let it. Alot of this it will be hard to understand but it is true . I use carriers all the time in my ministry I look for them so I can use there bodies to throw spirits in and out of the body,for the glory of the lord.With a carrier I can pull up any spirit from the dead it does not matter if they are in hell burning or sitting in heaven with the Father,yes it is real many of you have put a cap on the lord just limiting him to only what you read about him in the (HOLY BIBLE) he is much bigger than that I know because Im living proof.(GOD BLESS)

CHAPTER 15

Is it possible for your Love one's to live in your body after they are deceased ???

Once again it is Ordained by God for spirits to jump in and out of bodies,when someone dies that was not ready to die when they find out that they are allowed to jump in and out of bodies they just go crazy,because the first thing they want to do is jump in there love ones so that they can be close to them. I have seen it so many different times alot of people have trouble believing this until I proove it to them that there love one is inside of them as I keep saying threw this entire book that it is Ordained by God that they can do it. Now the reason God allows this to happen is because he is so (MERCIFUL) to the people and that also includes in death as well. Your love one can live in your body as long as your living trying to help you out in life by giving you strength and courage when you need it or they can try to destroy your life, by trying to take it over as it is there's. Now thats when I come into play with the spirit especially if its acting a big fool in your body Im the ghost buster,that chain them to darkness or I can send them to the light. Its according to if they love the lord or not,and if they show me respect for who God has me.There are alot of people just learning this information about what these spirits have been doing for years & years. they can really mess your up or help your life up,I know it sounds crazy but there is alot you don't know about God he's infinite and unpredictable,all day long.

CHAPTER 16

Angel's living out your life when you die is it possible ???

It is possible for Angel's from Heaven to live out your life in your body, and you yourself is dead you died some type of way, and the Angel assumed your life. I have seen it done many times and it was a shocker for me to see it, your family members will never know it they will live there entire earthly life thinking that your there sibling and your really a Angel from Heaven. Now let me answer the question you may have is why would God do something like that, the reason is number one he says in his word your ways are not my ways or your thinking is mine, that lets you know right there that he is very different than you and I so just have a strong open mindset or you will write off all this good information, in your fleshy body but when you die you will know that all this is not a holks it's what you need to be taking in so you can educate yourself on whats going on,on the other side of life.When this occurs the Angel that takes over the body does not all the time know that they are Angels,they are just following orders from the father whom we all love.It will not wrk if the angel knows where he came from,because it would conflict in everything that the angel has to do to lead a normal life style in that body. Remember the Angel has to blend in with everyone in this society thats why not having that memory of where there really from is wiped. Remember the scriptures in (HEBREWS 13.2) Be not forgetful to entertain strangers:for thereby some have entertained ANGELS unaware. This is a very true scripture I pray that you dont forget this scripture because Angels are here and they are not going anywhere.I gave you some names of people who did great things on this earth that were Angels that you did not know that they were Angels there lives were as good and complicated,to the point that you never even noticed. (Harriet Tubman the woman called moses)was a Angel of God. (Dr.Martin Luther King JR.) was a Angel of the Lord,look at the work that they did to save the people from the wrath of the devil. Many of you could possibly be living with a ANGEL as your love one or co worker or your local Pastor could be a Angel from heaven,I know it gives you alot to think about remember treat everyone equal God Bless.

CHAPTER 17

Sending spirits to the light to rest ???

My main job is to send spirits to the light where they can go and rest until judgement time. But the spirits that I send to darkness they wear chains in a dark place until judgement time. The reason God sent me was to police the spirits inside there bodies because without me,and other people like me these spirits would have there way in those bodies thats just one of the reasons the lord called me. Many Many spirits come to me for me to send them to the light,so they can go to rest some of them even say to me Prophet please send me to the light because Im tired and my feet hurt LOL. Now you can imagine hearing something like that it would just blow your mind,or make you think about whats really going on. All these spirits want to do is rest as everyone else want to do in the flesh it is my pleasure to send them to the light in the mighty name of (JESUS). alot of those spirits have been roaming since the days of Moses,and they are still roaming the local churches think that it is a ludacris thing to do when you are talking to the spirits but (JESUS) did it with lazarous,when he called to the spirit side and commanded the spirit to enter back in the body of Lazarous Amen. As I said I have met spirits from every time zone that there is from the 1500,s hundreds to the 2017 moment as we are in now. Nothing changes in the spirit real the only thing thats different is that you chose to educate yourself on this Incredible information. Most of your love one's are not resting in the light,they are sitting there looking and watching over you right now as we speak. Most of them are just sitting there living there spirit life out threw you and you may or may not know it, but just believe that the Lord loves you no matter what. Also dont just Limit yourself to just what you read in the Bible,because our God who is (CHRIST) Is a BIG BIG God...... I LOVE YOU ALL GOD BLESS.

ABOUT THE AUTHOR

Bishop James T. Johnson is a (SPECIAL DELIVERANCE PREACHER AND HEALER) He is also the owner and founder of Prophetic House of God International Ministries. Bishop is fluent in preaching,prophesying,Teaching, Mentoring,Casting out devils,Casting out spirits of dead people,Speaking to the dead,controling the dead.Teaching Reincarnation seminars.

In this book your going to be dazzled by the information, that your going to learn from this material,it exposes the spirits for who and what they really are.Just wanting to talk when you want to run from them,this book gives the dead a Big voice so that people may understand that they really have nothing to worry about the (LORD) has not forgotten you or them he has threw this bok educated you on his other side of his wonderful Holy spirit.

Bishop James T. Johnson

www.prophetichouseofgodministries.com

Email : bishopjohnson7777@gmail.com

P.O. Box 261.Wiggins,Ms. 39577

Printed in the United States
By Bookmasters